A Rainbow Book

D0913465

# Insects
# ON
# DISPLAY

## *A Guide to Mounting and Displaying Insects*

Connie Zakowski

## Library of Congress Cataloging-in-Publication Data

Zakowski, Connie, 1957-
    Insects on display : a guide to mounting & displaying insects / Connie Zakowski.
        p.cm.
    ISBN  1-56825-041-X (alk. paper)
        1. Insects--Collection and preservation. I. Title.
    QL465.Z35 2000
595.7'075--dc21

00-042526

*INSECTS ON DISPLAY: A Guide to Mounting and Displaying Insects*
© 2000 by Connie Zakowski

Publisher:
        Rainbow Books, Inc.
        P. O. Box 430
        Highland City, FL 33846-0430

Editorial Offices and Wholesale/Distributor/Retail orders:
        Telephone: (800) 431-1579
        Telephone/Facsimile: (863) 648-4420
        Email: RBIbooks@aol.com

Individual/Retail Orders:
        Telephone: (800) 431-1579
        Online from (http://www.)
            bookch.com
            amazon.com, and
            barnesandnoble.com

All illustrations and photographs by the author, Connie Zakowski

Manufactured in the United States of America.

Dedicated to the memory of my dad, Carl.
Also to my mom, Barbara,
my brothers, Steve, Brian and Tom,
and special friend, Celia.

Other books by Connie Zakowski

*The Insect Book: A Basic Guide to the Collection and Care of Common Insects for Young Children* (Rainbow Books, Inc.)

# CONTENTS

"One touch of nature makes the whole world kin."

— William Shakespeare,

*Troilus and Cressida*

*Insects On Display* was written to be a companion book to my first title, *The Insect Book: A Basic Guide to the Collection and Care of Common Insects for Young Children* (Rainbow Books, Inc.). *The Insect Book* describes how children can catch and keep many different insects. Because the captured insects die rather quickly, due to their short life-span, I wanted to give readers an activity to help preserve their collection.

This book describes what you need to know and the supplies you need to begin mounting insects in both box and dome settings. I have even included a few inexpensive substitutions for some of the supplies you will need to keep your insect-mounting projects affordable. My hand-illustrated, step-by-step instructions will demonstrate several ways to mount various insects. In this book I cover how to mount and display winged insects (butterflies and moths), hard-shell insects (beetles), and difficult-to-mount insects (walking sticks, flies, grasshoppers, katydids, and mantids).

Displaying mounted insects is a rewarding hobby that requires a fair amount of patience. It is an ideal hobby for the insect enthusiast, for the do-it-yourself crafter, for families looking for inexpensive hands-on activities, and for homeschooling parents who are looking for a great biology project for their kids.

Children need to learn the important role insects play in our planet's biology. For example, most crops would fail to produce food or seeds for new plants without the pollinating activities of insects such as bees. Other insects, such as fly larvae and termites, also function as garbage men that process animal and plant waste so it doesn't build up. Still other insects, such as mantids and wasps, hunt and eat insects, such as caterpillars, which destroy plants that produce food for humans. Collecting and mounting insects can evolve into a lesson for the entire family on how the natural world works.

Everyone in the family can be involved in collecting and mounting insects for display. For example, young children can catch and study common insects (see *The Insect Book*), gather background materials for dome displays, and decide upon insect positioning in action displays. Older siblings can dispatch insects, prepare them for display, and research information for each species. Parents can assist them in the construction of display boxes and domes, in the collection of background materials, and in giving rides to the library for research.

Even the most squeamish of family members can be involved in one or another of the necessary tasks, such as working with the display cases and coordinating supplies. Know too that insect collecting is an activity that families can pursue even on long, out-of-town road trips.

Because I have great respect for insects around the world, I would like to send readers a very important message: You do not need to kill every specimen you find, just to start your collection. To do that would be wasteful for two reasons. First, by capturing an adult insect or raising an insect from egg, larva or pupa, you learn much about that particular insect and how it lives, grows, and changes. If you simply catch wild insects without raising them from young, you lose the learning opportunity. Second, by killing too many insects in the wild, you could be helping make them rare or even extinct. Many species of insects are already endangered — some may even have disappeared entirely — due to mankind's continuing expansion into once-wild lands. New building construction and mankind's use of poisonous chemicals have put insects and other creatures in danger.

Whenever possible, I recommend that you let adult insects mate. I raise the same insect species from the eggs produced, and later release extra adults into the wild. That way, I help create more specimens of the species, instead of helping to destroy them. Some of the supply sources listed in the Appendix sell live insect specimens (and even dormant pupae and eggs) at various stages of development, so your hobby can be pursued at all times of year.

Whether this becomes a lifetime hobby or a onetime activity, the learning experience is fun and rewarding, especially if you choose to raise the insects that you plan to mount and display. I hope you enjoy using this guide in your quest to mount and display insects.

Connie Zakowski

# Supplies Needed

All of the items you will need to begin collecting insects for display may be purchased at your local hobby store. If your local hobby store does not carry some of these items, ask the manager if they can be ordered. If the manager is unable to order the supplies you need, you can refer to the Appendix to this book (page 59), which provides a list of companies that sell *entomological* (having to do with the study of insects) supplies. A mailing address, phone, fax, email, and website are given, as available, for each contact.

The following pages will describe each of the items you will need and, when possible, I have listed inexpensive substitutions. There are two different fluids used (dispatching and relaxing), triangle papers, a spreading board, pins, strips of thin cardboard, a Riker mount case, and a display mount case.

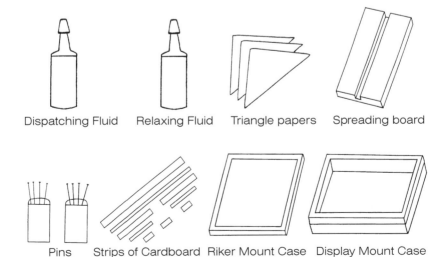

Dispatching Fluid    Relaxing Fluid    Triangle papers    Spreading board

Pins    Strips of Cardboard    Riker Mount Case    Display Mount Case

# Dispatching Fluid

### WHAT IT IS

Dispatching fluid is isopropyl alcohol (commonly called "wood" or "rubbing" alcohol). It is used to put insects, such as butterflies or moths, to rest. Young children should *not* be allowed to handle dispatching fluid; it is toxic, flammable, and an eye irritant.

### WHAT IT'S FOR

I use dispatching fluid mainly for moths and butterflies. It acts quickly and keeps them from fluttering around, which damages their wings. Butterfly and moth wings are covered with "scales" that get knocked off rather easily, especially when they are captured. Therefore, when you catch a butterfly or moth specimen, be sure to use the fluid on them right away.

> **A Close Up of Butterfly and Moth Wings**
>
> *For a really cool activity, look at a butterfly or moth's wing under a microscope or a very strong hand lens. Their wings are covered in "scales" that resemble shingles on a roof. These scales allow the insects to fly and give them color.*

### SUBSTITUTIONS

• *rubbing alcohol* (also known as wood alcohol or isopropyl alcohol)
• *fingernail polish remover* (also known as acetone)

### HOW TO USE IT

After catching a moth or butterfly, grasp it by the body so the wings are folded together. Squirt only a few drops of fluid onto the underside of its head.

Stay away from its wings because too much fluid could cause the

wings to get wet, which might discolor them.

Hold the specimen for a few minutes, then place it in a container or a folded triangle (see the next page). Keep it like that until you reach home and are ready to mount it (see page 23).

If your specimen is a female, it's quite possible that she may dispose of her eggs before she dies. The eggs will not be affected by the fluid. Carefully remove the eggs and place them outside in some weeds or bushes to allow them to hatch into caterpillars.

If you have captured or raised a specimen and you later want to mount it for display, you can place it in an airtight container. Squirt a few drops of fluid on a small, rolled ball of tissue or paper towel and place it in the container. The fumes of the dispatching fluid (or the substitute fluids) will be effective in putting the insect to rest.

---

### How To Keep Butterfly or Moth Eggs

*If you want to keep butterfly or moth eggs until they hatch, simply place them in a jar with a cover piece of cotton cloth, secured tightly with a rubber band. A cotton cloth allows air into the jar but won't let out any of the caterpillars, which are tiny enough to escape from screening when first hatched. Pull the cloth taut across the top of the jar, making sure there are no gaps (the caterpillars could get into any gaps, and they'd get squished when you take the cloth off).*

*Place a few twigs in the jar so the tiny caterpillars have something on which to crawl when they hatch. When you see the first of the caterpillars out, immediately put one large leaf (something the species likes) in the jar. You will soon see small chew marks. Follow the steps listed in* The Insect Book *for best results.*

# Triangle papers

WHAT THEY ARE

Triangle papers are papers used to keep specimens safe until it is time to mount them.

## WHAT THEY'RE FOR

Triangle papers are good for both butterflies and moths. After using dispatching fluid on your specimen, its wings can be folded together and it can be put into a triangle paper. Doing this will keep your specimen from getting damaged until you can mount it for display. Triangle papers can be purchased pre-folded at a hobby store.

## SUBSTITUTIONS

Some simple options to store-bought triangles are paper, napkin, paper towel or tissue. Obviously, the stiffer the material, the more protected the insect.

## HOW TO USE THEM

Begin with a square shape.

Fold the corner so it overlaps a bit on one side. Make the triangle a little larger than your specimen.

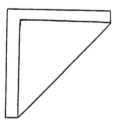

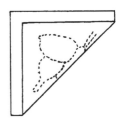

Place your specimen so that its body falls into the fold of the paper and its wings are closed together.

Carefully fold the top and the side flaps over. Place the specimen in a container until you are ready to mount it for display.

# Relaxing Fluid

### WHAT IT IS

Relaxing fluid (propylene glycol and hydroxyethyl cellulose) is a liquid that is used to soften stiff insect parts. It may be harmful if swallowed and it is a skin and eye irritant. Young children should *not* be allowed to handle relaxing fluid.

### WHAT IT'S FOR

Use relaxing fluid on a specimen that has been in your container for a long time, or use it if you find an already-dead specimen you'd like to mount for display. Relaxing fluid helps loosen legs and wings so you can position them in your display. Relaxing fluid can be purchased at a hobby store or from an entomological supplier.

### SUBSTITUTIONS

None.

## HOW TO USE IT

Using a container with no holes in the lid, place a folded piece of paper towel in the bottom and dampen it (do *not* soak) with relaxing fluid. Place your specimen on top of the moist paper towel and close the lid tightly. Leave it overnight, and the specimen will once again be flexible and ready to mount for display. If your specimen is still a little stiff, place it back into the contain until it softens. If you try to force stiff body parts to move, they will break off.

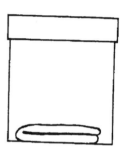

# Spreading board

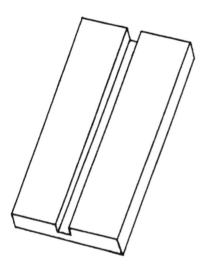

### WHAT IT IS

The spreading board is a piece of balsa wood (or other soft substance) with a section cut out of the middle.

### WHAT IT'S FOR

The spreading board has a pliable surface on which you can pin down your specimens. The groove in the center of the board is meant for the body of the insect specimen. Spreading boards can be purchased at a hobby store. When placing a large-bodied insect on the board, you may need to get an adult's help to make the center groove large enough to hold the body. A razor knife can be used to increase the width of the groove.

## SUBSTITUTIONS

Making your own spreading boards will require the help of an adult. Balsa wood or Styrofoam can be used to make your own spreading board. Buy a piece of balsa wood (10-12 inches long, 3-8 inches wide and ½ inch thick) and rout out a ¼-inch-deep by ¼-inch-wide groove down the middle of the board. Be careful not to cut too far into the wood or the board will easily break in half.

Options to the flat spreading board include a right-angle board that you can make by attaching two pieces of balsa wood using small nails or large stick pins. Put the boards together at angles to each other. This type of board is used with specimens that have wings. You mount them on this board when you don't want the wings to appear flat. Mounting them on this board gives them the look of an insect about to take flight, which might be appropriate for a dome display (see page 28).

If you cannot locate a hobby store to purchase the spreading boards, you can also use any size piece of Styrofoam.

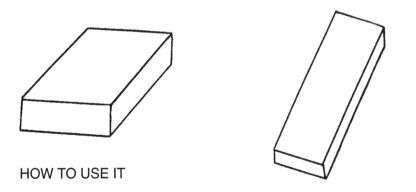

## HOW TO USE IT

This procedure is described on pages 36, 41 and 44.

## Insect Pins

### WHAT THEY ARE

Two types of metal insect pins are used when mounting insects: #3 and #0.

### WHAT THEY'RE FOR

The #3 pins are the sturdier of the two types and are used for pinning down the cardboard strips. The #0 pins are very thin, which makes them easier to push through your specimen. These special pins can be purchased only at a hobby store.

### SUBSTITUTIONS

You can use large stick pins that can be bought at a sewing center or in the fabric section of your local department store.

### HOW TO USE THEM

This procedure is described in chapters 3, 4, 5 and 6.

## Strips of Cardboard

### WHAT THEY ARE

Simple, thin strips of cardboard cut to various lengths and widths.

### WHAT THEY'RE FOR

They are used for holding specimens in place on a spreading board.

## SUBSTITUTIONS

If your local hobby store doesn't carry cardboard mounting strips, you can cut narrow strips from an old notebook cover.

## HOW TO USE THEM

This procedure is described in chapters 3,4,5 and 6.

# Riker Mount

### WHAT IT IS

A sturdy cardboard box, approximately one inch deep, filled with a smooth cotton batting, and topped with a clear piece of glass. It can be bought at most hobby or coin shops.

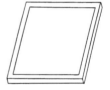

### WHAT IT'S FOR

This mounting case is designed for butterflies and moths.

### SUBSTITUTIONS

If your parents have a wood shop at home and like do-it-yourself projects, they can make you a simple case like this.

### HOW TO USE IT

After your butterfly or moth has been mounted, lift the cover off your Riker mount and place your specimen anywhere on the cotton. The cover presses the specimen against the cotton and holds it firmly in place.

# Display Mount

## WHAT IT IS

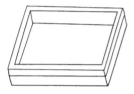

The display mount is a sturdy cardboard box, approximately two inches deep. The bottom of the case is made of pressed cardboard.

## WHAT IT'S FOR

Because of its depth, the display mount is used for displaying specimens that have a pin through them or for displaying insects that have a wide body or long legs (such as beetles, which would get crushed if placed in a Riker mount). There is no cotton batting in this case. You may want to add a drop of glue around the base of the pin so it stays more secure to the display mount bottom.

## SUBSTITUTIONS

Just as with the Riker case, your parents can make one if they have a wood shop and like to make things themselves. I would recommend that they look at a display mount at a hobby shop before trying to build one.

## HOW TO USE IT

Specimens are pinned to the bottom of the case. Since the bottom of the case is pressed cardboard, the pins are securely anchored, which keeps the specimen(s) from moving around in the case. However, be careful not to push the pins all the way through the bottom of the case.

# Body Parts

This is a reference page for the identification of the body parts that will be mounted and mentioned throughout the book. The three main body parts of all insects are the head (with two attached antennae, pronounced AN *TEN* EE), the thorax (like the chest of a person) and the abdomen (like the belly of a person).

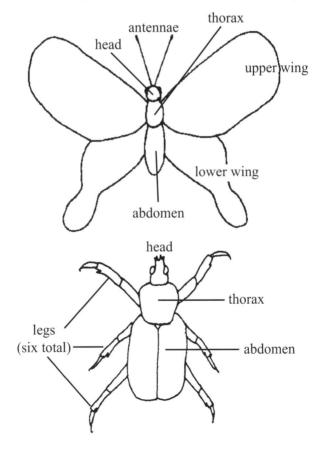

"The object of art is to give life a shape."

— Jean Anouilh,

*The Rehearsal*

# Mounting Butterflies and Moths

Before mounting your specimen's wings, you can draw lines across your spreading board with a ruler. This will assure accurate, square positioning of the wings. Measure from the end of the spreading board and use a pen to mark the spot. Draw a straight line across and repeat on the other side of the groove.

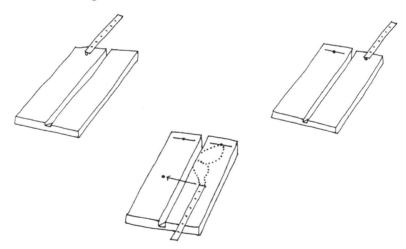

This is not a necessary step, but it will make it easier for the beginner to judge the position of the specimen's wings. The two straight lines will be used for this purpose.

Your specimens' wings will be different sizes, so you will have to measure from the bottom of the spreading board to the bottoms of the lower wings. You can do this after one side of the specimen is mounted. You simply measure the length, from the bottom of the wing to the end of the board, and use this distance to mark the other side of the board.

Try not to handle the specimen with your hands. The scales on the wings of butterflies and moths are like powder, and they come off very easily. Use the cardboard strips and pins to position your specimen into the groove of the spreading board.

## Mounting Procedure (for open wings)

### STEP 1

A butterfly or moth will usually die with wings folded together. Place the body of your specimen into the groove of the spreading board. Keep the tops of the wings near the measured lines (see the previous page).

### STEP 2

Select a strip of cardboard that is longer than the specimen's wings and slip it in between the folded wings. Using the strip, lay one set (either right or left) of wings against the spreading board. Place a #3 pin in each end of the strip to secure the specimen on its side.

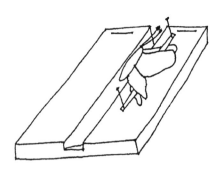

## STEP 3

Slide another strip of cardboard in between the folded wings. Slowly, using the strip of cardboard, fold the other set of wings over onto the other side of the spreading board. Pin down the ends of the strip. Note: The legs will be tucked underneath the body in the groove of the spreading board.

## STEP 4

Now that the wings are pinned down, you can position them to make them even on both sides. Hold down the end of the strip with your fingertip and remove the top pin. Put it through the top edge of the top wing.

Using the pin, move the wing to the line marked on the spreading board.

Place another pin into the top of the cardboard strip on that side. Then remove the pin from the wing. The first top wing is now positioned.

## STEP 5

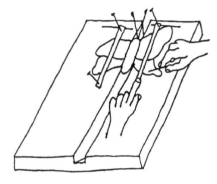

Position the lower wing using the same technique you used in Step 4 for the top wing.

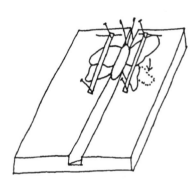

## STEP 6

Match up the other side of the wing, starting with the top wing. If you have a problem matching the lower wings, you can measure the length and mark the other side of the board.

## STEP 7

Once the wings are mounted, you may position the antennae. The antennae need to be laying flat, like the wings. Otherwise, they will break off when the butterfly or moth is placed in the shallow Riker mount.

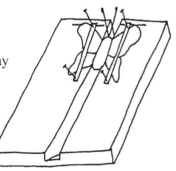

Use two small strips of cardboard and carefully pin each antenna down near the same-side wing.

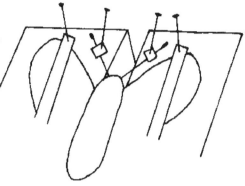

Leave your specimen mounted like this for a few days to allow the fluids in the wings to dry.

## STEP 8

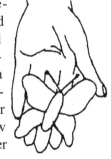

Carefully remove the pins, and your specimen will stay the way you positioned it. Using a pin, gently lift the specimen into your hand. Your mounted specimen is now ready to be placed in a Riker mount case.

## STEP 9

Lift off the cover and place your specimen on the cotton. Using a strip of paper, label the specimen for name, location found and date. Replace the cover.

## Mounting Procedure (for half-open wings)

To prepare a butterfly or moth for a display mount, you will need the spreading board that you have pieced together from balsa or Styrofoam.

The body of your specimen will be in the crease of the two boards instead of in a slot. Follow the directions for mounting your specimen to the flat board. Starting with Step 4 (see page 25), push a #0 pin through its thorax so the pin penetrates the crease of the board. This will make it easier for you to attach your mounted specimen to a flower or arrangement. Continue with the remaining steps for mounting the wings.

After your specimen has been pinned in this position for a few days, remove the strips of cardboard from its wings. Your specimen is now ready to be attached to a flower or to any type of arrangement.

# Mounting Hard-Shell Insects

Hard-shelled insects' legs tend to get stiff;      hard shell
therefore, such insects (mainly the beetles)
should be mounted as soon as possible,
especially if you don't have relaxing
fluid. Their thorax and abdomen are the
largest parts of their bodies, and both
are covered with a hard shell. The shell
over the abdomen covers and protects
their wings. Use a #0 pin to push through hard-
shelled insects' bodies.

## STEP 1

It is best to mount your specimen upside-
down to keep its legs intact.* The tiny claws
on its legs can stick to the spreading board
material and can be easily broken when you
attempt to lift it off the board. Therefore,
place your specimen, upside-down, on the
spreading board. Carefully push the pin
through its body, a little off to one side, until
you can see the end of the pin on the other side.
You want the pin to emerge a little bit to either side
of the centerline of its abdomen, because pinning it anywhere else can
cause its shell to crack or its thorax or head to come off.

* Mounting the specimen right-side up may be difficult since the legs may be hidden
  under and folded closely to the specimen's body.

## STEP 2

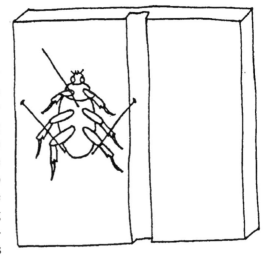

Extend the pin a little more so it will be able to stick into your spreading board. Clip the head of the pin with a wire cutter so it will stick into your display mount. Clip the head of the pin *only* if you are mounting your specimen upside-down. I prefer to mount specimens in the upside-down position because it makes the legs much easier to manage. Experiment to learn which way you prefer to mount your specimens. The clipped end of the pin will be sharp, so exercise caution when handling it, especially when mounting the specimen's legs.

## STEP 3

With the pin in your specimen, you are now ready to begin the mounting procedure. Place your specimen on either side of the groove in your spreading board. Using the #3 pins, place one against each side of the specimen's body to keep it from moving from side to side when positioning its legs. To avoid confusion, the three pins shown in this step will be omitted from the next **8** illustrations. Keep in mind, however, that the three pins shown are still there, holding your specimen to the spreading board.

## STEP 4

Mount one side of your specimen. Using a #3 pin, position the top leg. Slant the pin against the leg to hold it down.

## STEP 5

Next, pin down the middle leg on the same side.

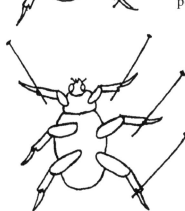

## STEP 6

Position the third leg and mount. After all three legs are mounted on one side, begin mounting the legs on the opposite side, taking care to match their positions to the already-mounted legs.

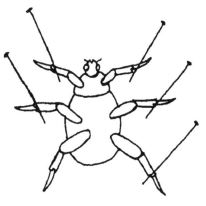

## STEP 7

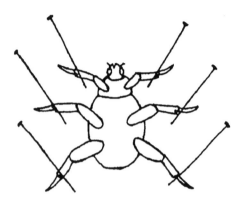

After all six legs are mounted, leave your specimen to dry for a few days. Once dry, carefully remove the pins. Your specimen should be stiff and ready for your display mounting case.

Even though your specimen is dead and mounted, check periodically during the drying period. Sometimes a leg will reflexively move from its mounted position. If this happens, simply reposition the pin.

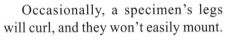
Occasionally, a specimen's legs will curl, and they won't easily mount.

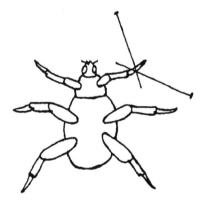

If this happens, use two pins to hold down the leg. Use as many pins as you need to evenly match each set of legs.

## STEP 8

Use needle-nosed pliers to secure the pin into the display mounting case.

CAUTION: Remember that the head of the pin was removed earlier. Using the pliers helps keep you from accidentally sticking the pin in your hand.

## STEP 9

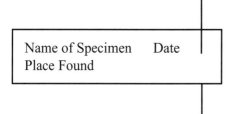

Name of Specimen    Date
Place Found

To label your specimen, simply write or type the name of the specimen, the place it was found, and the date on which it was captured. Place the strip of paper through the pin before securing it to the case. Keep the paper positioned close to the case and the specimen positioned close to the glass cover. That should allow enough room for the label to be read.

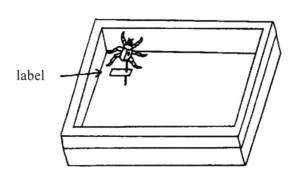

label

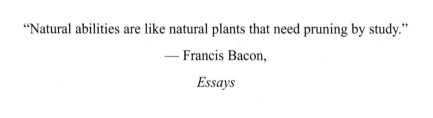

"Natural abilities are like natural plants that need pruning by study."

— Francis Bacon,

*Essays*

# Basic Mounting Procedures for Other Kinds of Insects

This chapter explains mounting procedures for other kinds of insects, such as flies, bees, wasps, dragonflies, grasshoppers and katydids. Almost all of these types of insects I mount in an upside-down position, except grasshoppers and katydids.

*clip*

*pin head*

**STEP ONE** (FOR MOST WINGED INSECTS)

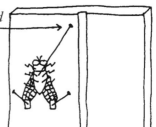

Clip off the head of the pin, as described on page 30. Using small pieces of cardboard strips, pin down the edges of its wings.

**STEP TWO**

Many times, the end of the specimen's abdomen will curl up (or down, from the insect's point of view).

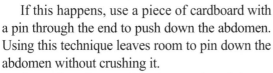

If this happens, use a piece of cardboard with a pin through the end to push down the abdomen. Using this technique leaves room to pin down the abdomen without crushing it.

Once the wings and body are pinned down, you can follow the leg-pinning steps found on pages 31-32. Be careful to avoid the extra four pins when mounting the legs.

## STEP ONE (FOR GRASSHOPPERS AND KATYDIDS)

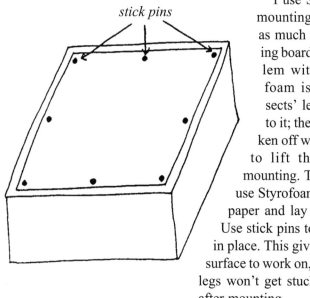

*stick pins*

I use Styrofoam when mounting insects almost as much as I use spreading boards. But one problem with using Styrofoam is that some insects' legs tend to stick to it; they are easily broken off when you attempt to lift the insect after mounting. Therefore, if you use Styrofoam, cut a piece of paper and lay it over the top. Use stick pins to hold the paper in place. This gives you a smooth surface to work on, and the insects' legs won't get stuck and break off after mounting.

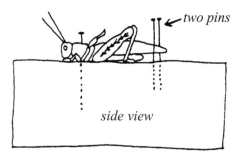

*two pins*

*side view*

*top view*

Styrofoam is best used for grasshoppers, katydids, walkingsticks and mantids. The light density of Styrofoam makes it easier to push in the pins unlike with balsa wood. Keep your specimen as close to the top of the pin as possible to allow room for its long legs. Use two pins at the end of its abdomen (one on each side) to hold it in place.

## STEP TWO

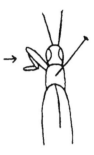

The legs of your long-legged specimen will be moved into a bent position, instead of the flat and extended beetle position. Mounting legs in a bent position can require three or more pins, per leg, to hold it in the correct position.

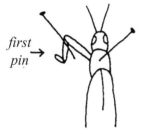

*first pin* →

The first pin is used to spread apart the first two segments, which naturally go into a closed position when the insect dies. Gently nudge the leg open and pin it in place.

*second pin*

The second pin is used to secure the leg and keep it from moving forward or down. Put this pin in a vertical position against the leg.

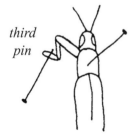

*third pin*

The third pin is used to hold down the tip of its leg (like your foot). You may need to use other pins if three aren't enough to position the leg the way you want it.

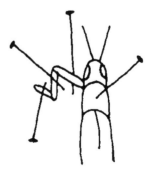

You can already see that you will use many pins — at least 18 if you use the minimum of three pins per each of the six legs (and that's not counting the pin in the thorax and the two holding the abdomen). Be very careful not to bump already-placed pins when mounting the other legs.

## STEP THREE

 The hind leg is usually the largest leg on a grass-hopper or katydid specimen. Mounting it requires the use of four pins.

As before, the first pin is used to spread the leg apart.

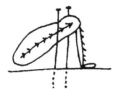 You will need two pins to secure the large part of the leg. You want to keep it from moving from side to side. Leave only a small space between the leg and the specimen's body.

Next, place a pin across the end, the tip of its leg (like your foot).

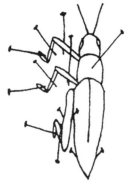 Mount all three legs on one side of the body before moving to the other side. When you mount the opposite legs, try to match the position as closely as possible to the first side you mounted.

## STEP FOUR

Leave your specimen mounted for a few days. Then carefully remove the pins. Your specimen is now ready for the display case. You may follow the options listed on page 33 for labeling.

## STEP FIVE

Katydids are mounted in the same manner as grasshoppers. Follow all the steps on pages 37-38. But because katydids' antennae are long, an additional step is necessary.

Using a medium strip of cardboard, stick a pin through the middle and bring the strip up, toward the head of the pin.

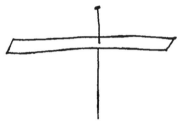

Gently hold the antennae up with your fingers.

Slip the pinned cardboard strip under the antennae and let them rest on the cardboard. Carefully pin down the strip of cardboard to the spreading board (or Styrofoam). This step will keep the antennae straight.

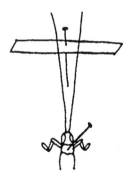

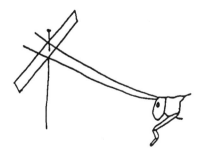

## STEP SIX

Leave your specimen mounted for a few days. Then carefully remove all pins except for the one you used for the antennae. When you lift up your mounted specimen, the antennae will lift off the cardboard strip. Your specimen is now ready for the display case. Follow the directions on page 33 for labeling your insect.

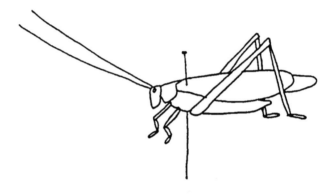

# Handling
# Difficult-to-Mount Insects

Walkingsticks and mantids are difficult-to-mount insects that require more pins than other types of specimens. All of their legs are large and long like the hind legs of a grasshopper or katydid. Their bodies are long and in the case of the walkingstick, slender. As a result, you will need to use more pins and cardboard pieces with difficult-to-mount insects. The first mounting technique described in this chapter will be for the walkingstick. The technique for the praying mantis begins on page 44.

### STEP ONE

Place a pin in the thorax (middle section) of its body. Mount walkingsticks on Styrofoam, and the pins will be easier to push in.  Remember to cover the Styrofoam with paper, just as you did when mounting the grasshopper.

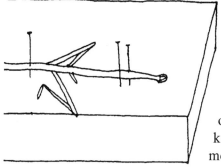

Leave a little room between the body and the Styrofoam. Don't press the walkingstick flat against the Styrofoam. Place a pin on each side of its abdomen (rear section) to keep it in its place while you mount the legs.

## STEP TWO

Place a pin in a tiny piece of cardboard and place it beneath the head of the walkingstick. This will keep its head from bending down. Push down the pin to the level at which you'd like the head to be. Mounting the head first keeps you from having to maneuver around the many leg pins.

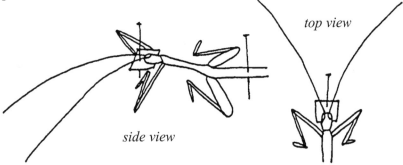

*top view*

*side view*

## STEP THREE

Mount the antennae in almost the same way as for the katydid on page 39. Remember to keep the cardboard you use for the antennae higher than the cardboard you use for its head. That way, the antennae will have a lifted, lifelike appearance when dry.

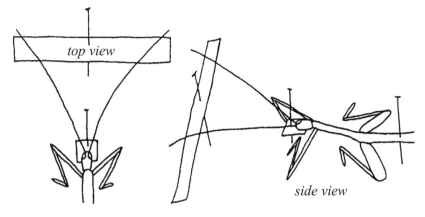

*top view*

*side view*

## STEP FOUR

Mount the legs using the same basic mounting procedures. Three pins should be enough to mount each leg.

Begin with the front leg. Spread the leg open and secure it with a pin.

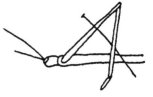

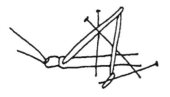

Next, stick a pin in between the leg and the body to keep the leg from bending inward. Secure the pin to the Styrofoam.

Finally, pin down the tip of the leg.

The next leg to mount is the other front leg. Once it is mounted, you can continue mounting the legs, alternating sides as you go.

## STEP FIVE

After a few days, remove the pins (except for those in the cardboard holding up the antennae and head). You may then carefully lift the insect by its main pin and place it in the display case.

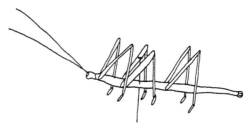

The praying mantis is one of the most difficult of all insects to mount. However, it is one of the most spectacular insects to place in a display, as its front legs are posed in a lifelike action position.

## STEP ONE

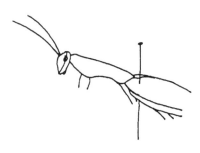

Using the Styrofoam block for mounting, center the mounting pin just below the thorax of the mantis and into the start of its abdomen. Be sure the pin comes centered between its legs. Because the mantis is a heavy insect, placing the pin in this manner keeps it more well balanced on the pin. Remember to cover the Styrofoam with paper.

## STEP TWO

After pressing the pinned specimen to the Styrofoam (don't press it flat), mount the first set of legs. The first two legs are the hardest to mount because they are very strong and usually closed tightly when the mantis dies. Use a strip of cardboard and two pins for

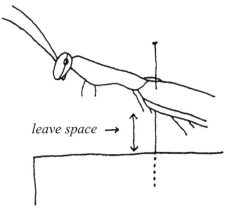

*leave space* →

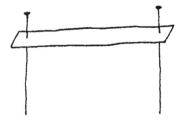

more support. Place a pin in each end of the cardboard strip. Push the cardboard up almost to the head of the pins. The end of the abdomen should be allowed to rest on the paper covering the Styrofoam.

Place the cardboard strip in front of the mantis' head and pin it down.

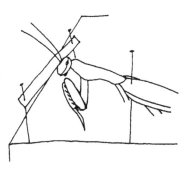

Use another pin to slip in between the folded leg. As the leg opens, carefully lift it over the cardboard "platform" that you just pinned down. Repeat the procedure for the other front leg.

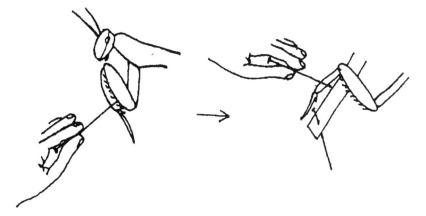

This is the top view of the front legs as positioned over the cardboard strip platform. Remember that the legs will not be bent outward like the illustration on the left; they will be bent down.

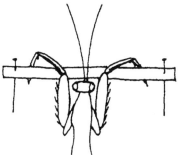

*bent down*

## STEP THREE

The head of a dead mantis bends downward. Use a medium strip of cardboard and one pin to hold up the head. You are making a little platform on which the mantis' head will rest. Use care when doing this step because this piece of cardboard goes over the top of the piece of cardboard you just placed under the front legs.

 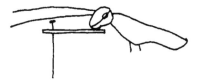

## STEP FOUR

Place another cardboard strip platform under the antennae, as shown on page 39.

## STEP FIVE

To mount the remaining four legs, refer to the procedure on page 43.

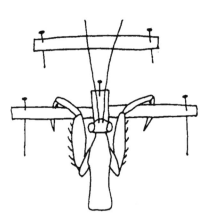

## STEP SIX

Remove the pins after a few days. Be careful when removing the strip of cardboard that supports the front legs. The illustration to the right is similar to the final result.

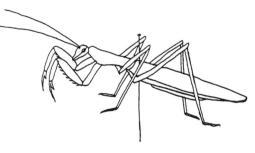

You have now learned the basic techniques for mounting almost any kind of insect specimen. The more you practice, the better you will be able to do it, and you will become a better judge of what each specimen will require.

You may discover different ways to do things or you may add steps. For example, when mounting the mantis, it is not necessary to open their front legs. But it looks more realistic to open them because they seem alive, ready to hunt. Some beetles have large mandibles (jaw-like structures at their mouth) that you may want to spread apart using pins. Moths have feathery antennae (butterflies have thin antennae with little knobs on the ends), which require extra care when pinning.

This hobby quickly becomes a favorite, especially with children and adults who like careful hand work. As you become more and more interested in mounting and displaying insects, remember my warning about collecting specimens: *Do not destroy every specimen you see.* Let nature take its course. Capture an insect, keep it at home, and feed it as long as possible (see *The Insect Book*). You will learn more, and you will see new ways to position it, by studying the specimen's actions while it is alive.

"The winds and waves are always on the side of the ablest navigators."

— Edward Gibbon,

*The Decline and Fall of the Roman Empire*

# Displaying Specimens in Domes

Using domes is a more creative way of displaying your mounted specimens. While Riker and display cases are best for displaying many insects in one place, the dome allows you to create a natural effect. You can use moss, artificial or dried flowers and other items that can make the insect look alive.

If you choose to use a dome, the following pages will itemize the materials needed, your options (when available), and step-by-step instructions for displaying and sealing the dome.

## Materials Needed

1 — Dome with base

2 — Hobby putty or
    florists putty

3 —Styrofoam shapes

4 — A bag of peat moss

5 — Artificial or dried flowers

6 — Clear silicone

7 — Aquarium sealant

8 — All-purpose glue or wood glue

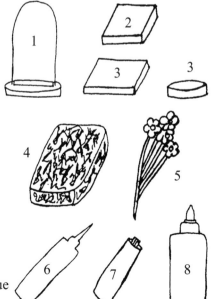

Domes can usually be purchased at a hobby, variety or garden store. Sometimes you can find them in the candle section (if so, they generally do not have a base). Some bases have a small pedestal in the middle and some have a groove already routed out.

Putty may be hard to find, simply because using Styrofoam is more popular. Both can be purchased at a hobby, variety or garden store. Find the one best suited to your purpose. The putty and Styrofoam are used for the base; they give you something to stick your diplay elements into.

Again, peat moss can be purchased at a variety, hobby or garden store. It is used to cover the putty or Styrofoam. By using peat moss, you create a more natural setting. The peat moss gives a grassy appearance to the bottom of the completed display dome.

Artificial flowers can be bought virtually anywhere. An option is to use dried flowers.

Clear silicone can be found at any variety store. Aquarium sealant can be bought at a pet supply store. Both items are used to seal the dome to the base once your display is completed.

All-purpose glue can be purchased anywhere. It is used to secure the pinned specimen to the flower or dried plant. It is also used to secure both the peat moss to the Styrofoam and the Styrofoam to the base.

## Assembling Your Display Dome

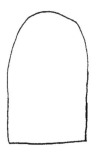  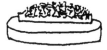

When using putty, spread it on the pedestal of the base. Taper the putty so it doesn't reach the edge of the pedestal. It will look like a mound. This will keep putty from smearing on the dome. Press the peat moss into the putty. With scissors, cut off any moss that hangs over.

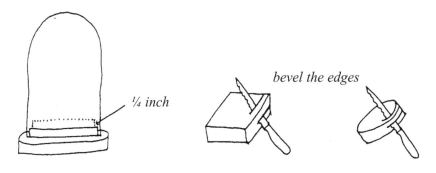

¼ inch          *bevel the edges*

When using Styrofoam, make sure the edge is at least ¼ inch away from the point that the glass dome makes contact. Whether using a square or round piece of Styrofoam, trim the edges to a bevel (a curve) by using a sharp knife (ask your parents for help with this step). By beveling the edges in this way, you will have enough room to cover the Styrofoam piece with your peat moss.

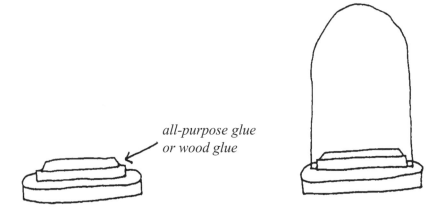

*all-purpose glue
or wood glue*

Make sure the fit of the Styrofoam is accurate, then glue down the Styrofoam piece to the base. Place the dome on the base to make sure the Styrofoam doesn't touch the glass. Remove the dome after checking, and allow the glue to dry.

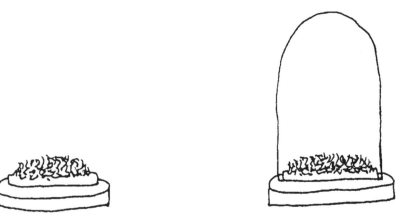

After the Styrofoam is secured and the glue is dry, put all-purpose glue, or wood glue, all over the top of the Styrofoam piece and cover it with the peat moss. Once again, place the dome back on its base to check for areas where peat moss has hung over. Trim any excess with scissors. Remove the dome and allow the glue to dry.

Your display dome is finished and ready for the mounted specimen. In my example, I used a mounted butterfly. Whatever specimen or type of flower or plant you use, follow the same instructions.

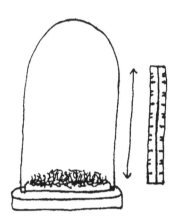 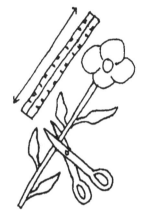

Measure the distance for the length of flower or plant you will need. Be sure to allow for the increased height of the flower or plant when your mounted specimen is attached. You do not want either the flower/plant or the specimen to touch the glass once the dome is placed on the base.

Place your flower or plant into the putty or Styrofoam. Replace the dome to make sure your measurement was accurate.

Hold the mounted specimen in one hand and pin it through the middle of the flower or plant. If the pin seems too long, carefully cut it using a wire cutter. Once your specimen is positioned, use a small dot of glue to secure the pin to the flower. Allow it to dry.

Once everything is set and has dried, clean the dome of any dust and place it on the base. Clear silicone or aquarium sealant can be used around the base of the dome. A small bead around the entire bottom of the dome will keep the dome secure and help prevent damage to the specimen.

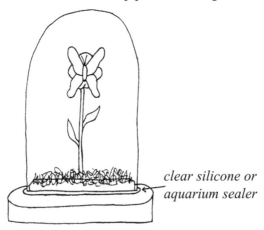

*clear silicone or aquarium sealer*

See the following pages for examples of what I have done.

# Display Examples

The following are examples of some of the Riker cases, display cases, and dome displays that I have made.

## Riker Mount Display case

# Display case

## Dome Displays

# Entomological Product Suppliers

**Hobby stores** — pins, cardboards, spreading boards, fluids, display cases, relaxing jars, triangle papers

**Variety stores** — domes, peat moss, artificial flowers, glue, silicone, Styrofoam, putty

**Sewing centers** — large stick pins, replacement cotton batting

**Coin shops** — Riker display cases

**Hardware stores** — balsa wood, glue, silicone

## ENTOMOLOGICAL SUPPLY STORES

**Australian Entomological Supplies Pty. Ltd.**
P. O. Box 250
Bangalow NSW 2479
Australia
Telephone: +61 (02) 6684-7650
Fax: +61 (02) 6684-7188
email: austento@nor.com.au
http://www.entosupplies.com.au
*Mail order supplies specialists established over 25 years. Provide books and equipment to both professional and amateur entomologists.*

**Ben Meadows Company**
P. O. Box 80549
Atlanta, GA 30366
Telephone: (800) 241-6401
Fax: (800) 628-2068
http://www.benmeadows.com
*Collecting and dissecting equipment, books.*

**BioQuip Products**
17803 LaSalle Ave.
Gardena, CA 90248-3602
Telephone: (310) 324-0620
Fax: (310) 324-7931
http://www.bioquip.com
*Entomological and botanical equipment, books, software.*

**Combined Scientific Supplies**
P. O. Box 1446
Fort Davis, TX 79734
Telephone: (915) 426-3851
Fax: (915) 426-3328
email: insects@overland.net
*Dead, dried insect specimens. 8500 species. "We have species nobody has."*

**Connecticut Valley
Biological Supply Co.**
P. O. Box 326
Southhampton, MA 01073
*Collecting and storage equipment, supplies.*

**Forestry Suppliers, Inc.**
P. O. Box 8397
Jackson, MS 39284-8397
Telephone: (601) 354-3565
Fax: (800) 543-4203
*Full catalog of field supplies and equipment.*

**Ianni Butterfly Enterprises**
P. O. Box 81171
Cleveland, OH 44181
Telephone: (216) 888-2310
http://iannibutterfly.net
*Best source for Imperial and Elephant brand insect pins; insect specimens, too.*

**Insect Lore**
P. O. Box 1535
Shafter, CA 93263
Telephone: (800) LIVE BUG
http://www.insectlore.com
*Educational materials, books, kits.*

**MORPHO v.o.s.**
P. O. Box 25 530 03
Pardubice
Czech Republic
Telephone/Fax: +42.40.24205
*Producers and developers of entomological equipment and accessories, nets, chemicals, pins, etc. Active in central Europe.*

**NASCO West, Inc.**
P. O. Box 3837
Modesto, CA 95353
Fax: (209) 529-6957
*Boxes, drawers, equipment and supplies.*

**Oliver Products Co.**
445 Sixth St., NW
Grand Rapids, MI 49504-5298
Telephone: (800) 253-3893
Fax: (616) 456-5820
http://www.oliverproducts.com
*Insect-rearing trays.*

**The Nature Store**
22 Charter Oak Court
Doylestown, PA 18901
Telephone: (215) 340-7693
Fax: (215) 340-7695
http://www.thenaturestore.com
*Books, entomology supplies, kids'
stuff.*

**Tropical Butterflies
& Insects of America**
6823 Rosemary Drive
Tampa, FL 33625-3980
*Catching and mounting supplies.*

**Ward's Natural
Science Establishment**
P. O. Box 92912
Rochester, NY 14692-9012
Telephone: (716) 359-2502
http://www.wardsci.com
*All kinds of supplies for biology/
entomology.*

**Wildlife Supply Company**
301 Cass St.
Saginaw, MI 48602
Telephone: (517) 799-8100
Fax: (517) 799-8115
http://www.wildco.com
*Insect-collecting equipment and
supplies.*

**Young Entomologists'
Society, Inc.**
Minibeast Zooseum and
Education Center
6907 W. Grand River Ave.
Lansing, MI 48906-9131
Telephone/Fax: (517) 886-0630
YESbugs@aol.com
http://members.aol.com/yesbugs/
bugclub.html
*Offers a large selection of entomo-
logical books and items for educa-
tors and students.*

## ENTOMOLOGICAL SUPPLY WEBSITES

The Internet is a great place to learn more about insects and find the supplies you need to capture, keep and mount specimens. Some of the more commercial sites also sell the finished display products that this book teaches you how to make. Examining these sites helps give you ideas for displaying your specimens, and it may help you find more exotic specimens than you can find in your own backyard. The following list will give you a start; however, you should also do your own search using Yahoo.com or your favorite search engine. If you do not have a computer or are not online, visit your local library, which may offer a library-patron computer that you can use to access these and other sites.

**Acorn Naturalists**
http://www.acornnaturalists.com

**Berkshire Biological Supply Company**
http://www.berkshirebio.com

**Bughouse**
http://15.net/bughouse

**Buginabox.com**
http://www.buginabox.com

**BUGS, Etc.**
http://community.webtv.net/bugguy2/BUTTERFLYANDINSECT

**Butterfly and Insect World**
http://www.insectnet.com/yoshi.htm

**Butterfly Art Creations**
http://www.insectnet.com/butterflyart.htm

**Butterfly Images of California**
http://www.butterflyimages.com

**Chinese Insect**
http://www.chineseinsect.com

**Chrysalid**
http://www.chrysalid.com

**Cicada Biological Supply**
http://www.cicada.co.uk/

**eHow: How To Start a Bug Collection (supplies available)**
http://www.ehow.com/eHow/eHow/0,1053,3842,00.html

**Entomology Discussion Groups**
http://www.entomon.net

**Entomology Interest Page**
http://www.rth.org/entomol/index.html

**The Insect Company**
http://www.insectcompany.com

**Insect World**
http://www.insectworld.com

**Insectes Mondiaux**
http://www.insect-trade.com

**Kendall Bioresearch Services**
http://ourworld.compuserve.com/homepages/kbservices

**Kunafin**
http://www.kunafin.com/English.htm

**Meissen Entomology**
http://www.crosswinds.net/~insects/meissenentomology/

**Newport Butterly Farm**
http://community-2.webtv.net/butterflyzoo/doc2/

**Quebec Insectes**
http://www.quebecinsectes.com

**Ronald's Roaches**
http://lonestar.texas.net/~rtremper/roach.html

**Russian Butterflies**
http://ww.osipov.org/insects

**Sericulum**
http://www.sericulum.com

**South American Insects**
http://insectnet.com/sa-insects.htm

**Wings and Things**
http://www.wingsandthings.com

**World Butterfly**
http://www.worldbutterfly.com

**The World of Insects**
http://www.insectnet.com/worldofinsects.htm

**abdomen** (AB doe men) — The rear part of an insect's body located after the thorax, similar to the belly of a human.

**antennae** (an TEN nee) — The pair of slender, movable sensory organs found on the head of an insect. One is called an antenna (an TEN ah).

**aquarium sealant** (a KWAIR ee um  SEEL ant) — A clear adhesive used to keep air or moisture out of your display case (and water and fish in an aquarium).

**bevel** (BEV el) — To slant the edge of a surface. Glass that has a beveled edge is less likely to cut you.

**clear silicone** (kleer SILL ih kone) — Similar to a sealant, a clear adhesive used to keep air or moisture out of your display case.

**entomological** (EN toe moe LODGE ih kal) — Having to do with the study of insects.

**entomology** (EN toe MOLL oh gee) — The study of insects.

**mandible** (MAN dih bull) — Strong jaws of the insect that hold or bite into its food source.

**mount** (mownt) — To set into position the insect's body parts.

**pedestal** (PED ih stall) — A base or foundation on which your display is mounted.

**pliable** (PLY ah bull) — When describing mounting materials, the word *pliable* describes 1] a soft surface into which pins may be easily inserted or 2] a surface that bends easily.

**specimen** (SPEH sih men) — One of many in a class or group.

**substitution** (SUB stih TOO shen) — Something used in place of something else.

**thorax** (THOR axe) The middle part of the insect body, similar to the chest of a human.

The following books will help you both identify your specimens and learn more about entomology, the study of insects. You can request any of these books from your local library. Use the ISBN number (a number that identifies a book and its binding) to help the librarian find the book you would like to borrow or to help the bookstore order the book.

## FOR CHILDREN

*About Bugs (We Both Read)*, by Sheryl Scarborough. Treas Bay Inc., 1999. ISBN 1891327070. (ages 4-8)

*Amazing Bugs.* Time Life, 1997. ISBN 0783548966. (ages 4-8)

*Amazing Insects*, by Laurence Mound. Random, 1993. ISBN 0679839259. (ages 4-8)

*Backyard Bugs*, Jennifer Stewart. Standard Pub., 1996. ISBN 07884710937. (ages ?-?)

*The Best Book of Bugs*, by Claire Llewellyn and Christopher Forsey. Kingfisher, 1998. ISBN 0753451182. (ages 6-9)

*The Big Bug Book*, by Margery Facklam. Little, 1998. ISBN 0316255211. (ages 4-8)

*Bugs, Beetles, and Butterflies (Puffin Science Easy-To-Read, Level 1)*, by Harriet Ziefert. Little, 1998. ISBN 0613113683. (ages 4-8)

*The Insect Book: A Basic Guide to the Collection and Care of Common Insects for Young Children*, by Connie Zakowski (the author of the book you're currently reading). Rainbow Books, Inc., 1997. ISBN 1568250371. (ages 6-10)

## FOR OLDER CHILDREN AND ADULTS

*The Encyclopedia of Insects*, edited by Christopher O'Toole. Checkmark Books, 1995. ISBN 0816013586.

*A Field Guide to Insects: America North of Mexico*, by Donald Joyce Borror and Richard E. White. Chapters Pub. Ltd., 1998. ISBN 0395911702.

*Guide to Observing Insect Lives*, by Donald W. Stokes. Little Brown, 1984. ISBN 0316817244.

*How to Know the Insects* (3rd Edition), by Roger G. Bland and H. E. Jaques. WCB/McGraw-Hill, 1978. ISBN 0697047520.

*The Insects: Structure and Function* (4th Edition), by R. F. Chapman. Cambridge University Press, 1999. ISBN 0521578906.

*Introduction to the Study of Insects* (6th Edition), by Donald Joyce Borror, Charles A. Triplehorn, and Norman F. Johnson. ISBN 0030253977.

*National Audubon Society Field Guide to North American Insects and Spiders*, by Lorus J. Milne and Susan Rayfield. Knopf, 1980. ISBN 0394507630.

*The Practical Entomologist*, by Rick Imes. Fireside, 1992. ISBN 0671746952.

# Index

## Connie Zakowski

Connie has taken you another step farther into the world of insect collecting. Just as her first book, *The Insect Book*, taught you how to collect and care for insects, *Insects on Display* has illustrated how to preserve your specimens.

Connie lives in southeastern Wisconsin, where summer months have provided her the opportunity to raise several insect species. Her most recent "family" consisted of Cecropia and Polyphemus caterpillars, which she raised from the eggs of mated moths of each species. Collecting all the food and caring for the caterpillars is time-consuming, and it kept her very busy. She enjoyed watching them grow, day by day. As summer comes to an end, the caterpillars will all make cocoons, and they will be returned to nature to spend the winter months in their natural environment.

During the winter months, when the insects are dormant, Connie spends her time creating displays of her specimens so they can be seen close-up for all the years to come.

Connie enjoys giving lectures and showing off her collection to different schools, youth organizations, and senior citizens' groups. During the winter, she brings her prepared displays; during summer, she brings live specimens. The reaction she receives from these presentations is rewarding. It always generates many entertaining stories of the viewers' encounters with the insect world.

The study of entomology has been an interesting and educational avocation for Connie. She still finds a little extra time for photography and plans to include this hobby in her future endeavors.